COMMANDING YOUR MONEY

FINANCIAL PROPHETIC
DECLARATIONS TO LIVE BY

DWANN HOLMES
ROSEMARY WINBUSH

ACKNOWLEDGEMENTS

Special thanks to our family, friends, church family, business associates, and clients for loving, supporting, and stretching us. We have had some good and not so good experiences when it comes to money. BUT it is from all these experiences we have learned and grown. We are *most* grateful to God for His Word and revelation as we have journeyed through all the ups and downs of life learning daily what He says about our living and our finances. We are honored to share what we have gleaned as it relates to commanding our money.

DEDICATION

This book, *Commanding Your Money,* is dedicated to anyone who wants to see a spiritual shift in their money matters. This book is for all those who are ready to change their thinking and prophetically decree and declare what God says over their finances. This book is for you if you want to see more of what God has made available through His amazing power and promises concerning money.

TABLE OF CONTENTS

INTRODUCTION

What you read in this book today will change your life forever. We are sharing insights, life experiences, and lessons we have learned about the power of God's Word and His promises concerning money and life. Make no mistake about it, God is the source of all things and His voice about everything should always be louder and more persuasive than anything else with no compromise. We are not professional financial advisors, but we walk in faith and are spiritual advisors with biblical, Christ-centered principles that bring unmatched promised results. If we follow what God commands, we will see results. The problem is we have trouble believing and being obedient to the

Author of Truth. There comes a point in our lives we have to decide whether or not we are going to take God at His Word and follow His ways. You will read some of our stories, which are all true, but our testimony is we had to fight to trust and act on our faith in God's Word. We had to fight to change our mindset about His Word. We had to speak and act on what the Word said to see the manifestation of the promise. We came to the deep understanding that our words truly frame and form our world. Once we learned the tactics of warfare rooted in our *mindset*, we went into battle better prepared. So, this book shares both tactics and strategies to fight and win when it comes to your money. Let the Word do the work and affirm what it says about your money.

Our stories are a part of our spiritual money mindset transformation. As we put obedience and trust into practice, we experienced an overwhelming confidence in God and our mindset towards Him changed. It is truly like being a child trusting God, our Father, at every corner. We searched the scriptures to find out what God says about money; then we put it to the test *believing in our hearts* it would happen. As your mindset changes, your soul will prosper; and as your soul prospers, you prosper.

As you read each declaration and the stories we share, examine your own mindset to see where your thoughts and your heart reside when it comes to money. What are you saying about money? Are you speaking negative, positive, or even what God says? Do you let others dictate your money position based on their thoughts about what you can and cannot have? Do you fight doubt, or do you let it become the victor? Are you willing to change your mindset to operate in a *'covenant money'* realm? Do you have a giver's heart?

Remember, money is a medium of currency used to create an exchange in market spaces. It is a physical, virtual, and digital commodity for a spiritual and earthly purpose. It is a means of earthly exchange for a heavenly reward. Access to God's *'currency'* may be unorthodox (Matthew 17:24-27), so open your mind to prophetic declarations and expect the supernatural power of God to work on your behalf.

What we do with money is a reflection of our hearts. Our wealth is not just for us and our pleasures, but it is for the good pleasure of Kingdom purposes. Don't be a lover of money but be a lover of what money can do in the hands of a true servant of God.

Before we dive into the power of *Commanding Your Money*, we must share some foundational principles we believe make all this possible. When you understand how systems work, you also understand how systems don't work. These principles are a necessary part of manifesting what we are sharing. They are principles we had to accept to prophetically declare these promises over our finances. They are principles we live by which open heavenly gates, so distributions can be made to all of us who choose to believe and have great expectations.

When much is given, much will be required in faith, obedience, and sacrifice, but there is an exchange rate that far exceeds our comprehension. Putting into practice what you are about to receive is not from us, but from God. It is His divine order of generating wealth and great provision. God gives seed *(money)* to the sower *(giver)* for the benefit of sowing *(giving)* into what is beneficial for the Kingdom. Positioning yourself to be a giver will position you for more to give. It is *"Abba"* Father's Will to bless His children who are willing to listen to His instructions and follow His plan and purpose.

FOUNDATIONAL PRINCIPLES

The earth is the Lord's, and everything in it...the world and all who live in it (Psalm 24:1). Everything belongs to God, but He has given mankind access to His divine treasures through favor and grace. We are allowed, through the kindness of God, to participate in His creation as family and stewards. As family, we have entered into a covenant adoption, through Jesus Christ, and become heirs to the Kingdom of God. We have become citizens of God's Kingdom which operates in the natural and the supernatural realms. We function in the government of two worlds, one being superior over the other. As stewards, we have been given authority and dominion over the movement,

8

management, and establishment of God's possessions in the earth as He has disbursed. This means our faith in God's authorization as His sons and daughters *(family)* to possess, occupy, and rule must be real in our thinking and in our actions.

Within this universe, there are principles and laws established by God to demonstrate His power and His glorious authority which is unchanging and unmatched. When we understand these principles and laws, we are able to function within them as benefactors of what they offer.

There are spiritual laws as well as natural laws. *'You shall reap what you sow'* is one of these laws we can use in many areas of life, but our thinking of where we plant *(sow)* is how we will harvest *(reap)*. We attract what we expect through our thinking and our actions. What we **think** about and where we put our strong focus will determine our expectancy level when it comes to our declarations concerning a thing (Proverbs 23:7). So, guard your thinking.

If we cooperate with these principles and laws of God, we will be fruitful and prosper. We can manifest the power of God's Kingdom through our obedience and trust in Him. God's principles and laws can take root in our consciousness and subconsciousness. When this happens, what we *think* about and the possibilities of what can happen will shift our mindset and our actions.

We do not give money to get money, but we give with a passion to please God; then we can embrace the expectation to receive what God has promised. Obedience to God produces fruit and blessings (Malachi 3:10 – Bring all the tithes into the storehouse, That there may be food in My house, And try Me now in this," Says the Lord of hosts, "If I will not open for you the windows of heaven And pour out for you such blessing That there will not be room enough to receive it.). We don't have to worry about our needs and wants, because the Lord will provide. If we seek first, the Kingdom of God and His righteousness, we will receive the blessings of what is needed and even desired when we delight ourselves in the Lord (Matthew 6:33; Psalm 37:4).

It is not because of the measure of what we have given, but because of our willingness to give all, we can expect God to keep His Word. We are family and stewards who passionately want what God wants. We give because it is the desire and character of our Father in Heaven. We give to continue the ministry of Jesus Christ, to make sure those who lead and serve in the work of Christ are cared for, to give support to those in need, to further the vision of God's Kingdom, and to do what God requires. We do it with our time *(valued commodity)*, talent *(capacity)*, and treasure *(finances)*. The seeds we sow should be a sign that we are coming into agreement with what God says about sowing.

The Bible has over 2,000 scriptures about money. This means God has something to say about money...its use and the results of its use. Our tongue is a creative force, and we too should pronounce what God says about money. The Bible says there is power of death and life in the tongue (Proverbs 18:21). The words we speak over any situation are a reflection of how we think and what we expect. Do not destroy your seed's direction by killing it with your tongue. We must guard our words over our money and speak well over what we desire our money to accomplish. Faith without works is dead (James 2:17, 26)...so, if we have faith and do nothing with it, it is dead. If we speak nothing over our money, it is like death and weakness to its efforts.

As you meditate on each word in these ten (10) declarations, allow your mind to be renewed, allow yourself to rediscover the power of God, and remember the promises of God concerning the obedience of giving and receiving. Create a strategy to speak over your giving. Point and direct how your seed will produce a harvest. See, in advance, the testimonies to be produced from your giving. Determine where and how your seed will produce. *Where* – where will you plant your seeds and *How* – how will you target your seeds to produce a specific type of fruit. Remember, fertile soil produces more and better fruit; and certain fruit generates greater income power in a market, so plant well.

Commanding things to happen puts you in a position of authority and control. The world will put a demand on your money if you won't. Without strategy, planning, and purpose, the power of the money afforded to us to possess is not maximized for Kingdom efforts. *Commanding Your Money* means you have the ability to speak over your money before money gobblers attack. Money gobblers grab your money before you can put it towards efforts of purpose. There are so many testimonies about people coming into large sums of money only to waste it away, because there was no spending strategy for spiritual and earthly purposes.

Being able to command puts you in a place of advantage. About 85% of people in the world live in a place of surviving when it comes to money. We are here to tell you there is more than surviving. We want you to thrive and God wants you to thrive. God has plenty for His people, and every follower of Jesus Christ should know that.

Each declaration is an expectancy based on the promises of God. The word 'I' combined with a state of being *(am)* or action word *(tithe, sow, give, expect, believe)* simply puts us in a place of affirming who we are and what will happen when we step into what we are affirming and decreeing.

We are givers and have seen the blessings of obedience and surrendering. There is an old song by Doris Akers, and it says, 'You can't beat God giving, no matter how you try.' This means no matter how much we are blessed to give; God can always top it in His giving. He wants to give to His children for His purpose. As you embark on elevated principles of *Commanding Your Money*, watch and see the glory of God manifest in your life.

As we express to God our heart's desire to give, He will provide the seeds to give, which will not only bless us, but the purpose to which we are giving. Start *Commanding Your Money* as soon as you read the following **Offering Declarations**. Decree it often. Be ready to fight the thoughts of attack, and see yourself victorious in giving and receiving. Each time you plant a seed, ask God to remember your sowing, then wait for the harvest. In real life, a harvest takes time to grow and mature. Sometimes it can be the same in a spiritual way, but sometimes it can be a *'suddenly'* type of harvest. However God decides to manifest can be a part of your expectation and faith. It is your Kingdom responsibility to share your testimonies of *Commanding Your Money*, because others need to walk in this same flow of giving and receiving.

As you say each declaration, take time to decree in your own words what Holy Spirit is revealing to you about what you need to gain and let go of in order to have a transformative spiritual money mindset. Work with the declarations and not against them. Make the necessary adjustments in your life to give and to receive what God puts in your hand as a sower. Put into practice what you hear from God, and be confident in His Word and His voice. Develop a deeper prayer life and commune with The Lord always. Lay down your old ways of unhealthy thoughts about money and pick up God's wealthy thoughts about money. Remove the fear of not having enough, and stretch your mind to visualize more than enough. Meet God at a place you have never been before. Ask Him to bring you up higher, and be willing to go all the way with

Him. Now, let's start *Commanding Your Money*!

OFFERING DECLARATION

1. I'm a purposeful Believer who gives on purpose.
2. I'm a cheerful giver and a cheerful tither.
3. I tithe expecting God to rebuke the devourer.
4. I sow my seeds expecting a divine harvest.
5. As I give, I expect to live in abundance.
6. I expect to be a lender and not a borrower.
7. I expect overflow in all I do.
8. As a child of The King, I expect to experience heaven on earth and divine harvest in:
   - Jobs,
   - Contracts,
   - Land deals,
   - Real estate,
   - Bills paid,
   - Houses paid off,
   - Cars paid in full,
   - Debt free businesses and living in divine wealth and health.
9. I believe the blessings of the Lord makes me rich and adds no sorrow.
10. In Jesus name.

DECLARATION 1

I'm a purposeful Believer who gives on purpose.

2 Corinthians 9:8
And God is able to make all grace abound toward you, that you, always having all sufficiency in all things, may have an abundance for every good work.

Do you know why you give? Is your initial intent in giving to please God?

God is the author of giving. He has given us His only Son, Jesus. He has placed us in His creation and sustained us. When we can truly see His giving towards us and the purpose it has in our lives and in the lives of others, we understand the power of giving on purpose. If you have received something with a purpose

23

behind it, it means more. It could solve a problem and create ease in your life and in the lives of those around you. Getting or giving for a cause brings reward to both the giver and receiver. God wants to *give* just as much as we want to *receive*, but He wants to do it His way. Whether we learn to stand in the wind of faith and pronounce what we want or surrender our own will unto God's Will, God is ready to bless us. There is a cause and effect of faith and obedience which bring financial and transformational rewards. Coming into agreement for supernatural blessings changes our mindset about how we see God and His ability to produce what others are not willing to see. Be a Believer who gives with the recipient's purpose in mind, and be a Believer who gives with your own harvest purpose in mind.

Declaration 1 Journey
The Pizza Test - Dwann Holmes

Life and death are in the tongue and the power of our words are the fruit of life. As a leader in the Kingdom, it is my responsibility to help others have the right mindset when it comes to sowing. I did not know what people in my reach would be dealing with from week to week, so I wanted them to have something they could speak over their finances on a regular basis to declare the power of God concerning increase, so I came up with the *Offering Declaration*.

In 2006, my family was dealing with some financial challenges, and we knew we needed more income. I remembered listening to Dave Ramsey. He said if you need extra money, go get a job at Dominos and you'll make more money than you think you can. So, I jumped on that idea and got a driver's job with Dominos. Yes, I sure did. I remember thinking to myself, how I needed to practice what the Word says about declaring what I wanted concerning my money. So, I thought this would be a perfect opportunity to do so.

I wanted to test the Word, so on one of my deliveries as I got out of my car to deliver the pizza, I thanked God for a $20 tip and when I got to the door, that's exactly what I got...a $20 tip.

I thought to myself, this really works. So, I did it again! And it worked again! So, I continued to declare things over my finances, and I watched God perform in ways I couldn't imagine. This was one of my first *'documented'* experiences of commanding my money, and I will never forget it. Now, no matter how small or big the financial need I always open up my mouth and prophesy to my seed by commanding it to come forth. You can too! Try it today!

Declaration 1 Journey

Crying and Trusting - Rosemary Winbush

In 1995, I was faced with making an employment decision that would test my trust in God relating to our family financial income. In 1993, after the birth of our first child, I went back to work in corporate America. I enjoyed my job and the people I worked with. I saw myself as an individual who added value to the company and envisioned career growth and longevity with the company. After the birth of our second child, I thought about working part-time with the idea I could go back to the company after the children were a little older. The company I worked for was so gracious towards me that they allowed me to work from home and come into the office occasionally. It was what I thought to be the *'perfect'* set up. But on this particular day, I remember it as clearly as if it was yesterday. I was driving to the office to drop off some paperwork, and I heard the Lord say, 'I want you to leave this job and stay at home with your children. I will take care of you, and I will bless your husband so your salary will not be missed.' I began to weep, because I really knew the Lord was speaking to me. I did not want to leave my job and all I seemed to have worked so hard for, but I knew I had to obey God. That evening when my husband came home, I told him what the Lord spoke to my heart. Being the man he is, he humbly said, "well I guess we have to do it." The rest is history. While others were being laid off at my husband's job, he was getting promoted. The financial blessings grew, and he not only got my salary in his income, but bonuses too. When you know you *"really"* heard from God, trusting Him and His promise will bless you more than you will ever know.

These *Declaration Journey* stories were stories of faith and obedience. We all have been tested in our faith and obedience to God. However, the outcome will depend on our decision and choice. We can make a decision to have faith in what God says, but the choice to implement what is necessary to complete the decision is up to us. Faith and obedience are like partners who bring or create increase and blessings.

Decree that you give with a purpose of Kingdom growth. Decree that you intend to be a part of God's plan in the earth, and you will use money for this effort. Declare Heaven is coming to earth through your giving. Declare you are a Believer assigned to sow and seed will be given to you for this purpose. Declare you are obedient to God and trust Him in all things.

Declaration 1
Write your personal strategy to give on purpose and record your outcome story.

DECLARATION 2

I'm a cheerful giver and a cheerful tither.

2 Corinthians 9:7
So let each one give as he purposes in his heart,
not grudgingly or of necessity; for God loves a
cheerful giver.

*Is your heart dead to the joy of giving? Are you
pressured to give or is it a pleasure to give? Do
you know giving is the character of God?*

Why is parting with what *'really'* doesn't
belong to us so challenging. If you haven't
looked at it this way, you might want to. If we
believe the foundational principle that all things
belong to God and He has the power to give and
take away, it changes our perspective about
giving. Remember, we are stewards, which
means short-term possession with a surrender

35

policy. When we are blessed to be a blessing, there can be great joy in the act of being used for God's plan and purpose. A cheerful heart draws in the Spirit of God and creates an atmosphere of abundance. Being cheerful in giving is tied to our prosperity. Attitude matters to God, and the right attitude in any situation produces opportunities. God notices the manner in which we give and our cheerfulness in obedience gets His attention.

Programmed behavior can create artificial joy, but a pure and genuine heart experiences real joy and connects with God. Operate in the oil and spirit of cheerfulness when you give.

Declaration 2 Journey

Not Really Ours - Rosemary Winbush

My husband had just received a commission check and he wanted to buy something he wanted, but God said not yet. We got a call from a close relative who needed bail money. At first we were disappointed and contemplated what to do, but we surrendered the funds. We learned that our wealth was not just for us, but it was given to us because God could trust us to be *earth fund movers*. When we become fixed on what we want to do and not the source of Who the pipeline flows from, which is an unlimited source, we are not useful to His cause. A few months after we were able to help our family member, God blessed us with more than we gave. Sometimes God gives us something for someone else. He knows the timing and He knows how much. Don't think what you have really belongs to you. This way it's not so hard to give it up. We didn't get repayment, but God took care of us, because He had a plan. There is a caveat to this idea and that is there's more where that came from, and it doesn't run out.

I once asked the question, 'is it okay Lord for some of your people to have so much' and His answer was a very quick response, 'yes if they release back to Me when I call for it.' At the same time I knew if it was not given when called for, it would only be a period of time when it may be given to another who God would use. I have heard many stories told by God's people about being told to give what seemed to be big ticket items. They talked about the fear of giving and then the fear of God's hand if they were disobedient. They realized it was divinely given to them in the first place, and they knew God could do it again and do it to exceed what He had done before. I truly know this, and I give with a cheerful heart.

Declaration 2 Journey

Let It Go - Dwann Holmes

Sometimes God will challenge you to be cheerful in giving something you love. Back in the early 2000s, I had a baby blue BMW 318 that I absolutely loved. It was paid off and looked great, especially with no car payments. My production company also owned a DODGE CARAVAN which was decked out in our company logo and motto, when wrapped vehicles were not all the rage. While at church one day my family learned about a single mother who desperately needed a car. She had more than a few kids and was routinely catching the bus. The thought crossed my mind to give her the car. We discussed it as a family and knew it was the right thing to do. After all, we had more than enough. My office was five minutes from the house and the Dodge Caravan was sturdy and reliable and yep, paid off too.

We decided the best thing to do was to partner with a local ministry and donate the car with instructions for that ministry to give the car to the young single mom.

As a family we were cheerful in giving this and never once regretted sowing the car. It was a season where we chose to let it go, knowing it is indeed a blessed occasion to be able to give to someone in need.

These *Declaration Journey* stories deal with understanding, at a higher level of stewardship, what it means to surrender what God requires. God is so gracious to let us use what He has allowed us to steward over. When He commands release, we must release. It is important to know when God speaks to your heart. Do not confuse His voice with compelling voices. When His plan is at work concerning what He desires, we must trust He will not abandon His promise to the faithful.

Decree you enjoy giving and it brings you great joy to give. Declare you will not allow fear, stress, or apprehensiveness to keep you from giving. Declare anger, frustration, or loss will not rise up when it is time to give, but cheerfulness and appreciation to give will be the champion of your giving. Declare you will release when it is time to release, because you draw from an unlimited storehouse.

Declaration 2
Write your personal strategy to become a cheerful giver.

DECLARATION 3

I tithe expecting God to rebuke the devourer.

Malachi 3:11
And I will rebuke the devourer for your sakes, So that he will not destroy the fruit of your ground, Nor shall the vine fail to bear fruit for you in the field," Says the Lord of hosts;

What poor decisions trap your seed? What can you do to protect your future harvest?

Money gobblers represent the devourer. What's eating up your money? What money pests are you dealing with? Could it be unwise spending, overspending, or even underspending.

45

Unwise spending results from not planning on what you spend and sometimes disobedience. Writing the vision applies to your money too. If you don't have a plan, the enemy will create one for you. If you want to command your money, you must take authority concerning it.

Overspending might be a part of spending what you don't have to spend and spending more for something than you should. Buying on credit *(money you don't have)* can lead to money destruction and digging a pit taking unnecessary energy and effort to get out of. Overspending on things that cost more than you have can really put you in the same pit. Be wise and seek wisdom, so you don't overspend. Trust God for the things you desire and wait for His divine opportunities to receive them.

Underspending means you invest in necessary items of poor quality for fewer dollars. This causes you to reinvest costing you more money, because you didn't save or initially invest with wisdom. You can suffer the hard knocks of underspending by reinvesting in the same thing over and over again.

Position your money for purpose. When you receive what you asked God for, quickly put it towards that purpose. You have to move faster than the money gobblers of unwise spending, overspending, and underspending. If you put it where it's purposed to go, you secure it for that purpose.

Declaration 3 Journey

Asking and Receiving - Rosemary Winbush

When our children were little we prayed for their future, from God blessing them with spouses who loved Him to how we would pay for their college education. My husband is such an amazing father and an amazing steward of our family. He told me in his own prayer time, he was talking to God about how he wanted to make sure our children had the opportunity to go to college and have no debt being a slave to student loans. He had gone to a conference and saw a businessman who sowed his entire commission check. He thought to himself, I would like to do that. That very same year, God answered the prayer. He received a commission check and we agreed to sow the entire check. God continued to be faithful. Shortly after this, my husband received another commission check which paid for all three of our children's college tuition. When we received the money, we immediately put it in a college plan to ensure those money gobblers could not eat our harvest. We knew it had a direct purpose, and we could not risk any of it being wasted on what it was not intended for. God gave us wisdom against the devourer. Sometimes the devourer comes disguised as another need, and we are tricked in unpurposed direction of our harvest simply, because we forgot why we asked God for it or something else conveniently slips in to take over. Then we go back asking God again for what He has already provided for the solution. The devourer will cause us to not intentionally use what God has given us for the purpose we asked. This is how we are even deceived into thinking God did not respond, and we shortchange praising and thanking God for his wonder-working power of great provision. Unfortunately, we repeat these cycles without even being aware we need to be delivered from misdirecting our money.

Declaration 3 Journey

The Power of the Tithe - Dwann Holmes

Early in life, my parents instilled in me the principle of tithing. It was taught at church and demonstrated in my home. However, it wasn't until I accepted my first TV NEWS job in Savannah that I really saw the POWER OF THE TITHE, for myself.

I was a young assignment reporter making a whopping $17k a year. I was living with a roommate who worked with me at the station in an apartment in a huge house downtown, not far from the station. After paying my tithes and my bills, I was a bit uneasy knowing I literally had almost nothing in my bank account. How could this be? If I remember correctly, I knew I needed gas and some food, and it looked like I didn't have money for both.

I thought to myself this is what *'testing'* is about. I went to work the next day, and when I got home, there was a card waiting for me on the table. It was from one of my mom's dear friends and family friend, Carol Jackson. In the card to my delight and surprise, there was a check that would carry me over until I got paid.

That was a money memory and miracle I knew I would never forget. And it proved to me that as long as I gave my tithe and worked the Word, God would work on my behalf.

These *Declaration Journey* stories demonstrate an awareness of purposeful asking and purposeful distribution. When we ask God for something specific or He even knows what we need and He obliges, we must follow through with the direction of the provision. This type of awareness teaches us God cares about specificity and our needs. Even though there is plenty in His storehouse, we must be integrious with our requests and follow through. If we don't apply the blessings to the pinpointed request, we run the risk of the devourer coming in to rob us of the gift of praise, the fruit of honesty, and the proper use of the harvest.

Decree you are a tither, and your seed will not be devoured, but will flourish in its purpose. Declare no weapon formed against your money and your possessions will be able to prosper. Declare your money is protected, and it will complete its assignment.

Declaration 3
Write your personal strategy to guard against the devourer encroaching on your money territory.

DECLARATION 4

I sow my seeds expecting a divine harvest.

Luke 6:38
Give and it will be given to you: good measure, pressed down, shaken together, and running over will be put into your bosom. For with the same measure that you use, it will be measured back to you.

Do you picture your harvest? Is it big or small? Do you understand the capacity of your harvest flows from an unlimited river source?

For this purpose, divine is something coming from God like a miracle. These are the blessings we can't explain, or we didn't see them coming like they came, but because we have a mindset of being in a constant posture to receive, we expect a blessing in every situation and around every corner. Wherever we go, in every situation, we expect to be blessed. We sow from a heart of obedience and joy knowing sowing and reaping *(giving and getting)* is a spiritual law with promise. Therefore, it is under God's divine order to bless the sower, and He will even give seed to those who choose to be called a sower. The revelation is this, if you position and define yourself as a sower before you even have a seed, you will receive a seed to sow. That's a reverse blessing mindset; be a giver in your heart and mind first and then you will receive seeds to sow.

Declaration 4 Journey

Back Child Support - Dwann Holmes

After years of being lenient with my daughters' father regarding our original child support agreement, I decided it was in the best interest of my girls to go through the legal system. As the girls were growing up, I was flexible when their dad wasn't able to help at the level that he should have. Yet God still took care of us. However, there were some lean years that we had to pray through. Then after calculating all the missed payments and recognizing that Florida had no statute of limitations on past due child support, I knew I had to swallow my pride and move forward.

During that time, I never would have imagined it would take exactly one year for everything to come full circle. Even though I clearly had all the paperwork, it seemed like week after week the system was requesting something new. It was taking so long to see any relief that I began to get very disappointed. But I knew I had to press through not just for myself and my girls but for others who needed to be encouraged in what God would do. Not only did I command those funds to come through, but I believe this was a part of me and my daughters' harvest for all the seeds that had been sown in the past and also reciprocity for what had been lost over all those years that I didn't necessarily fight for.

Right before my yearly Holy Prophetic Convocation, which always happened during the season of Yom Kippur & Rosh Hashana, I received news that indeed the order had been corrected and monthly funds would be coming through. To my surprise, almost a year later around the same time right before convocation again, even though it showed that there were substantial funds that had been released in March, they didn't show up until September. Nevertheless, this situation proved to me that indeed God watches His own.

Declaration 4 Journey

Expect the Unexpected - Rosemary Winbush

I can remember reading God's word and saying to Him, Lord I want to be a sower of more; I want to give to people; help me to be able to give. Not only did I speak these words, I told the Lord I wanted to be able to give a specific amount. Once the sincerity of my heart was sent up like sweet perfumes to the Lord, He gave the exact seed to be sown with overflow. Because of our hearts desire to be givers, there are blessings around every corner.

My gas story (propane) is just one of many that my husband and I have experienced. When we

62

positioned ourselves to adopt the attitude that God is truly working things out for our good, we learned that patience, kindness, and diligence accompany the manifestation of the blessing. For almost three years in a row, we would order gas from the local gas company and each time they dropped fuel, they would *(for a divine purpose)* put more fuel in the tank than we ordered. When we got the bill, we called to let the company know it was an incorrect order. Because of their error, we received free or discounted fuel of hundreds of dollars. When dealing with the company, we remained calm, we were patient, and we were diligently looking for a blessing. Our expectations to receive a blessing created an atmosphere to obtain it. It was hard to believe the same error on the same account would repeatedly happen, but GOD ALLOWED it to happen as a blessing to us.

I'm amazed that some people don't see dollars in the form of discounts, coupons, in-kind, etc. If you add it all up in a year's time, this type of divine harvest can add up to thousands of dollars. So, don't allow blinders to be pulled over your eyes thinking God is not at work in all situations. The enemy will try to disguise your blessings, so you won't see what God has done. In each situation, we could have been angry, mad, and frustrated, which by the way are all blessing blockers. We could have been taken out of the place of having that high level of expectancy to see blessings in their true form.

These *Declaration Journey* stories reveal our ability to see God at work in His divine promise to bless the sower and even to provide the seed to the sower. Think about how you think. Our expectations are a reflection of our ability to receive what God has for us. Having a heart to give will create an environment and provision to give. When you expect a blessing around every corner, you must be patient and demonstrate the character of God to receive it.

Decree you recognize your harvest is from a divine place and has The Glory attached to it. Declare nothing can hinder what is sent from God which is divine. Declare you daily expect the unexpected blessings of The Lord. Declare that your seeds carry a weight to attract divine things. Declare you are prepared to receive a heavenly harvest for an earthly good.

Declaration 4
Write your personal strategy to believe in your divine harvest.

DECLARATION 5

As I give, I expect to live in abundance.

2 Corinthians 9:6
But this I say: He who sows sparingly will also reap sparingly, and he who sows bountifully will also reap bountifully.

How is your living? Do you plan to live in abundance? Do you operate in a wasteland?

We are dealing with expectations again! The life of a believer is not to live in survival mode, but to live a *'more'* abundant life. We are positioned for abundance, because it is, again, a promise (John 10:10). It's not what we are saying, it is what God is saying in His Word. So, raise the bar and shift your mindset that abundance is your portion.

69

Psalm 37:25 says, 'I have been young, and now am old; Yet I have not seen the righteous forsaken, Nor his descendants begging bread.' We are the sons and daughters of The Most High God and joint heirs with Jesus Christ, therefore, we are a blessed people. We are a people of abundance. Receiving this in your heart changes everything. When you are royalty, you are royalty with certain rights and privileges. You can ignore your birthright if you want to, but you still have unused access to the birthright. We are saying come into the mindset of your birthright and use it for Kingdom advantage.

Declaration 5 Journey
Back at You Blessing - Dwann Holmes

I believe you have to get to a point in your life as a Believer where you truly understand we are called to live in abundance and not lack. But you have to literally EXPECT abundance in all that you do. I call it, God's prophetic economy at work.

I remember during the first prophetic convocation that I hosted, one of the main speakers agreed to come and to just sow into what God was doing. But I also heard God tell me to give a $500 seed from my personal funds. I did so expecting that indeed I would receive a harvest as well. That's the abundance of God. And literally within the same hour someone sowed the same amount into me. I believe that's a sign of God's abundance and overflow in our lives. Before we can even release a seed, God is already orchestrating on our behalf to prophetically allow us to receive what we sowed. Now, remember the Word says, 'as long as the Earth exists, there will always be seedtime and harvest,' and I truly live by that. In order to walk in our harvest season on a regular basis, we've got to be willing to sow on a regular basis and know that the fields are right for the Harvest.

This *Declaration Journey* story has a power message. The expectation is based on knowing who we are in the Lord and what type of lifestyle we are supposed to want and walk in. When we understand this principle, we will want more, so you can give more; and when we give more, we will receive more.

Decree that abundance is your lifestyle, and you acknowledge who you are as a child of God. Declare that nothing will come in the way of your abundance thinking. Declare that your mind is set on a more abundant life in all areas of your living. Declare you dwell in a place of giving and you expect abundance in knowledge, understanding, opportunities, provision, health, wealth, etc.

Declaration 5
Write your personal strategy to change your mindset to live a more abundant life.

DECLARATION 6

I expect to be a lender and not a borrower.

Deuteronomy 15:6
For the Lord Your God will bless you just as He promised you; you shall lend to many nations, but you shall not borrow; you shall reign over many nations, but they shall not reign over you.

Which will God call you...a lender or a borrower? Is your wealth condition positioned to lend?

Get out of the borrower's seat and slide over to the lender's throne. Being a lender means you have the resources to lend. Prophesy over yourself that you are a lender, and then expect people to come to you asking to borrow. Do your heavenly due diligence to decide if God is

76

instructing you to give to certain people. Always handle things with godly wisdom. When we step into the mindset of a godly lender, we know our resources come from Godly provision. Pray to be a lender and have the heart of the sower. The position of a lender gives you access to testify to the ways of Jesus Christ to the borrower. So, do not look down on the borrower, but help the borrower find ways to escape the chains of borrowing and to keep their word to repay.

A borrower is an individual or entity that takes or uses something that belongs to another individual or entity and agrees to pay it back. The only difference between a borrower and a thief is they agree to pay it back. We can all attest to individuals who borrowed money from us and didn't pay it back. They took something that didn't belong to them and didn't give it back. It sets them up to be a *form* of a thief. Being a borrower is not something God wants for His elect, because it can possibly trap us into becoming a *form* of a thief.

In our society, we are subjected to extreme borrowing, because it's a way to make extreme money. If you have to borrow, remember it is not to be your way of life.

Proverbs 22:7 says, 'the borrower is a servant to the lender.' If you have large amounts of unsecured debt (i.e., credit cards, personal loans, etc.), get a strategy to break the chains of money slavery. While you are coming out of these chains, don't have a gloom and doom mindset, because it will put you in a mindset setback. Wherever you are, get a strategy TODAY to get out of debt. There are all sorts of tools to help you calculate a plan of getting out of debt. You might have to seek out a reputable resource for advice. Like the street committee says, 'if you don't know you better ASK somebody.' Your strategy to get out of debt should be refreshing, because you have made a decision to do it. What took you time to get into, *may* take you time to get out of. However, have faith that God can do anything, anytime, and any way He sees fit.

Declaration 6 Journey
Asking to be a Lender - Dwann Holmes

In the congregation where I am the lead pastor, we were releasing this part of the declaration each time we gathered. After a season of making this declaration, one of the members said someone asked to borrow $30. They were speaking this as if it was not appropriate for the person to ask them to borrow $30. I reminded them that this is what we were decreeing...to be the lender and not the borrower. Then I asked if they were able to lend the money and with hesitation they told me at first they were not but changed their mind and did lend the $30. They quickly forgot what we were decreeing and as it manifested, they were not conscious of God positioning them to be a lender. Our expectations to believe God hears us and keeps His promises are sometimes in a dry place. When we shift our expectations to a *'land of milk and honey,'* we will be ready to walk in the words of what we declare and decree without fear or reservation.

Declaration 6 Journey
When I Got It - Rosemary Winbush

There are times when something happens, and God jolts you to remind you of His Word. A friend of ours was in a tight spot and needed a large sum of money. They had been a person of integrity and good standing in many ways. At the time we were able to help them, and we did with their promise that repayment would be made within 30 days. We felt what we would loan them would not be missed for just 30 days. The friendly transaction was made; and all we had to do was wait until the 30 days were up, and we would have our money back. When it was time to pay up, there was a problem. They didn't have it to pay back and asked for an additional week. We said we understood and agreed to wait. The week went by and still no funds. I was getting a little distressed and started talking to the Lord. I heard, *'I've made you the lender and not the borrower.'* I almost choked. I had to repent, and say thank you Lord, so sorry. I GOT IT!! I sat for a moment to assess what He wanted me to do. It was...*just wait*. I waited and I didn't harass the person. About two weeks later, I received a call to arrange a pickup time for the payment. Our agreement didn't include any interest or special *'pay me back this amount'* type thing, just a friendly loan. I could tell our friend was somewhat embarrassed about not paying back on time. She said she was so grateful we helped her out of a jam, that she wanted to just bless us with a little extra. It was far above what we could have expected. Because of obedience to repent, be patient, and wait, God blessed us. Sometimes God gives us funds to help others who may need to borrow. When we obey His voice, our attitude towards His heart will benefit us in some fashion.

These *Declaration Journey* stories give us an *'aha'* moment when we realize this declaration has been fulfilled. When we actually recognize ourselves as lenders rather than borrowers, it shouldn't be a surprise. We can really believe God is a rewarder of those who take Him at His Word. It's a process in the mind and the wallet to become a lender. The steps we take to get there require a level of commitment on our part to see it through.

Remember, it's not that we lend to any and everyone, but to the ones God instructs us to. We are not foolish lenders, but we are wise obedient lenders. Never look down on those who borrow, because we will always have those who borrow among us. We have probably all been in the borrower's seat, but we are taking these declarations seriously to make the shift. We have the mindset to declare which one we will become. Put in place the desire to become a lender.

Decree you are a lender who follows God's instruction to lend. Decree you are not a slave to the borrower. Declare your provision will be used to bring some out of borrowing and into lending. Declare your strength comes from lending and not borrowing. Declare freedom from debt is your portion. Declare once you are set free from debt, you will not go back.

Declaration 6
Write your personal strategy to become a lender and leave being a borrower.

DECLARATION 7

I expect overflow in all I do.

Malachi 3:10
Bring all the tithes into the storehouse, That there may be food in My house, And try Me now in this, "Says the Lord of hosts, "If I will not open for you the windows of heaven And pour out for you such blessing That there will not be room enough to receive it.

Can you measure overflow? If so, what does it specifically look like to you?

Putting God to the test is not a place of disrespect, but a place of finding out who He is and experiencing the power He possesses. Do we really believe what the Word says, or do we just say it? Putting it into action demonstrates our true faith in God's Word. Even if we think it's foolish, unorthodox, or mocked by others, God is saying try Me and see who I AM. His Word is true and there is nothing too hard for God (Jeremiah 32:27). As a matter of fact, with God all things are possible (Matthew 19:26).

Declaration 7 Journey
It Keeps Coming - Rosemary Winbush

Wherever I go, I expect to be blessed! Yes, I expect to be blessed, and I expect to be a blessing. I expect people to give to me, and I expect to give to others.

I was traveling to a church conference with a friend many years ago, and while we were in the airport for a layover, we decided to have lunch. She mentioned to me I'm hanging with you, because you attract blessings. During our lunch, the waiter forgot part of the order, so the manager came over to the table to check on us, and he asked about our travels. We told him we were headed to a church conference. We had a great conversation, and I prayed for him after we talked. For some reason, people always tell me their life story...I guess it's a God thing. After our conversation, he decided our lunch was *on the house*. The prayer was my giving to a person who needed someone to speak into their life with confidence in the God we serve. Sowing prayer was an exchange for a blessing from my Father in Heaven.

I never think about it, but I realize I have an expectation that is built in my DNA that I know God is going to bless me. I expect discounts, fees being waived, upgrades, special considerations, free stuff, etc. These things among others all add up to overflow.

Now is a good time to test your expectations. Expectations work with patience, kindness, love, and wisdom. What you are expecting may take time, so be patient. What you are expecting may require you to have empathy, so show kindness. What you are expecting may demand you to be an expression of Jesus Christ, so love others as you love yourself. What you are expecting, may require you to guard your tongue, so exercise wisdom. All these concepts represent the character of God and from His character there is a reward of overflow.

This *Declaration Journey* story reveals the test and power of our expectancy to receive overflow. Walk in a level of expectancy that attracts Kingdom blessings. Be confident not in yourself, but in the God you serve. Around every corner there is a blessing waiting for you. There is a blessing with your name on it. Claim it with your ever-growing mindset of expectancy.

Decree you stand under an open Heaven, because your mind is open to great expectations. Decree you have excessive surplus that you alone cannot accommodate. Declare that your overflow will be a blessing to not only you but to others. Declare that all you put your hands to will prosper and generate overflow.

Declaration 7
Write your personal strategy to expect overflow.

DECLARATION 8

As a child of The King, I expect to experience heaven on earth and divine harvest in:
Jobs,
Contracts,
Land deals,
Real estate,
Bills paid,
Houses paid off,
Cars paid in full,
Debt free businesses and living in divine wealth and health.

Proverbs 3:9-10
Honor the Lord with your possessions, And with the firstfruits of all your increase; So your barns will be filled with plenty, And your vats will overflow with new wine.

Do you believe <u>some</u> of the things on this list are possible for you? Or do you believe <u>all</u> are possible for you? Do you believe anything is *too hard for God or Do you believe He can do anything?*

We declare freedom and breakthroughs are coming to your financial portfolio. A new way of seeing what God will do concerning His promises is being established in your heart as you consistently work on *Commanding Your Money.* Our giving creates an overflow of our vats *(being)* with new wine *(new way of thinking).* As a child of The King, expect His promises concerning you are *yes* and *Amen.* God says *'yes'* to you having possessions as we honor Him with them.

This declaration covers so much of what many might say are only possessions, but it's much

98

deeper than that. It's about possessions, but it's about promises. God promises good and perfect gifts come from Him. He would not give His children a serpent if they asked for a fish (Luke 11:11). When we use jobs, contracts, land deals, real estate, being debt free, and living in divine wealth and health as testimonies, it brings glory to our Father in Heaven. When He is the One who orders our steps, we pronounce Him as the One who did it all. When others *hear* AND *see* what God is doing in the lives of those who operate in His Kingdom principles, they will want to know more. This opens the door to lift up the name of Jesus, so others will be drawn to Him, and THIS honors God.

Declaration 8 Journey
Relief From a Battle - Dwann Holmes

Trusting God for our children's future takes prayer and planning. When you think you have a plan, and the plan includes agreements made with others, it can get a little sticky. Hear me well. Things don't always turn out the way we plan, but they will work out because of God's plan. Before my children were getting close to college age, I planned to have provisions for them to attend college. It was an agreement between me and their father, my ex, to work together to ensure the continuing of their education. Unfortunately, that was not the case. After long battles and discussions to get support, I found myself winging it and getting my oldest to work to help pay for her education. Don't get me wrong, there's nothing like learning the value of a dollar and developing a good work ethic and learning the importance of investing in yourself. I did it and know plenty of others who did it. But the plan was we would both help our children. Of course, time for college rolls around quickly when life is happening. So, my oldest finally gets off to college, but then a few semesters down the road she has to take a break because finances get tight. After being faithful to work and save, keeping up her spirits, and having a desire to press on, God answers prayer! Unexpected blessings are when we know God is at work. When money comes from places you never thought about or didn't think was possible, it does. My mother decided to share some inheritance early! It was enough to pay off past-due tuition and get her back in school.

When you continue to expect God to move, expectation will give access to portals for poured out blessings. I believe our prayers, consistent declarations, and expectation to get back in school, bombarded heaven and activated Kingdom principles to bring forth what we needed.

Declaration 8 Journey
Going BIG - Rosemary Winbush

Don't be intimidated to ask for what you really want. God can handle it. Nothing is too big or too small for Him. God had given me and my husband the same dream around 1999. It was a dream to build a home with a training facility onsite. This was a promise from God where we would be able to share His wisdom with others through the teaching gifts He placed in us. So, my husband and I made a decision to sell our home to test the water. Our realtor friend helped us price our home and it sold quicker than planned. I'm sure some of you know what that's like. There was panic and excitement at the same time. In less than 30 days, we had to find another place to live which was kind of scary. With three kids in tow, we knew we had to find something quick. My husband traveled a lot for work, so I had to scout out suitable properties to look at with him when he was not traveling. I remembered there was a new subdivision that was being built nearby. This meant the same schools and same general neighborhood, which was a good thing. I knew it was going to be a temporary home, so I checked it out. There seemed to be only homes being built and that was going to take some time, which we didn't have. I sat in my car at the subdivision management office, and I prayed. The next day the property manager of the subdivision called me and said they had decided to sell a model home if we were interested. It was a four bedroom, two bath home and fit the needs of our five member family. So, I told them to hold it, and we would come back as soon as my husband returned from traveling. When he came home, we dashed over and grabbed it! The price was right, and we lived there for two years while building a new home.

But let me jump back a little. After we had the dream and before we put our house on the market, we were looking for land to move forward on the dream. The Lord impressed on my heart, that when we saw it, we would know it. Unfortunately, we did not see any properties that met the dream description, but we kept looking. Then I heard a quiet voice saying, *'Not yet.'* I said to the Lord, 'what should we do?' Answering in the way He does, *'I will give you something for now.'* Then I said, 'show me Lord, I know it won't be the promised land, but give us a good deal.' We found a double-sized lot in the same subdivision where we sold our house. There was no for sale sign on the lot, but I researched to find the owner and with a little detective work, I was able to locate the owner. When I called the owner, I found he was an older gentleman. He told me he and his wife purchased the land with the intent to build, but his wife passed away and there was a possibility he would sell. So, he said, 'make me an offer.' I wanted to be fair and at the same time not overpay. So, we made a serious offer. When I gave him a number, he accepted. He told me many people wanted to purchase the property, but he would not sell because he felt they were trying to take advantage of him. He said some people were insultingly low and some would never give him a number. He said he was selling to us, because we made a fair offer. I thanked God for wisdom, because I treated him the way I would have wanted to be treated. So, we got the lot, knowing it's still not the promised land.

Now back to the new subdivision home purchase. We purchased the temporary home and began to build on the lot. As we were building, God was showing us how to work with and hire a builder, how to sketch out floor plans and work with an architect, go through what seemed like millions of steps in the building process and even work with financial bank draws. I now know what God has in store for us. Back then we weren't ready to take on a huge building project. What we have learned is God scaled it for us to teach us. There were some pretty ugly things that happened in the building process, but we learned what to do and most importantly, what not to do. After building this home, our business operations are run from it, we've hosted small training sessions, allowed others to stay with us who were doing ministry, and benefited financially from all of it. God is still training us for what will come, and we are being attentive to the steps and strategies He is putting in place. So, ask for what you want, and God will prepare you for it and bless you along the way. Stay tuned for the vision fulfilled.

These *Declaration Journey* stories show us how God will keep preparing us for what is greater. The worst thing we can do is step into a promise too early and not be prepared or equipped to handle the magnitude of what God wants to give us. When God brings Heaven to earth we need to be ready for it. Maturity in the government of God is far above the riches of this world, because it brings sustainability and effectiveness. When we step into the BIG Visions of God, we need a BIG mindset to keep it going. All of what we are doing to pray, get closer to The Lord, practice in the teaching of Jesus Christ, and submit to the guidance and power of Holy Spirit, God will make us ready in His timing.

Decree you are of royalty as a child of The King, and it cannot be underestimated. Decree that Heaven is coming to earth for you. Declare you have possessions that honor our Father in Heaven. Declare that your freedom from debt will promote your blessings of wealth. Declare that your decisions are a reflection of your position as a child of God which will determine what you experience as a Believer.

Declaration 8
Write your personal strategy to visualize what more of heaven on earth looks like.

DECLARATION 9

I believe the blessings of the Lord makes me rich and adds no sorrow.

Proverbs 10:22
The blessing of the Lord makes one rich, And He adds no sorrow with it.

Are you afraid of what wealth will bring with it? Are you a real candidate for wealth?

Your position as a child of God makes you a candidate for wealth with no sorrow or shame attached to it. There should be no sorrow when we are blessed by God. Jesus came to break the curse of poverty, because sorrow is attached to it. Sorrow is a very deep state of distress absent of joy. Joy is our portion even in wealth.

113

Sorrow in wealth can come from thinking it's too much to handle and causes great stress. It will require something from us to manage money and wealth...to whom much is given, much is required. But it is not a burden, because God is the burden bearer. It will not add sorrow, because God said HIS blessings add NO sorrow.

Sorrow in wealth can also come from the voices of others if we give them access to our heads. Many times, we can let other people dictate how we feel and live in the blessings of God. They use words like, 'why do you need a bigger house or a better car, why do you want to send your child to that college, you're an overachiever, you're like us and don't think you're better, that won't work for you, no one wants what you have to offer, they'll never go for that, don't waste your time, that costs too much money, broke people can't think like that, you'll never be able to make it happen, just be comfortable where you are, you have enough already, just take what you got and be happy, you don't want that kind of stress, don't get your dreams smashed again, that's for the rich folks, that's too much for you, etc.'. These words are mindset killers. Ignore them and take hold of the mindset disruptors we are giving you. Don't hate the people who said it, but hate the effects of what was said. Dig deep to uproot all of the negative mindset killer spells casted upon you, because their results are companions of fear and doubt. You have the ability to choose and believe what God says. Remember, God's Word should *super rule* over all other voices.

Declaration 9 Journey
The Right Voice - (from both authors)

We have experienced over and over again people telling us about how their family members, friends, and co-worker make them feel uncomfortable about the blessings of The Lord in their life. Our comments are always, 'never to be ashamed of the blessings of God.'

Being ashamed of the blessings of The Lord is like having an ungrateful heart towards what He has given. God loves a grateful heart and an ungrateful heart He despises. Pleasing God is more important than pleasing people. If we allow others to dictate our emotional posture concerning the blessings of God, we are allowing their voices to occupy a space only intended for Him.

Prosperity runs in your race, and it fits you like a tailored garment. When you try it on, it feels good. There will always be others who will have a negative comment on how you look and how things fit. But, because you like it, it fits you well, and it costs you something, you wear it anyway. Do the same when it comes to your blessings of wealth. God has given us the land rights of the earth. We are the authoritative stewards over the earth and that includes the gold, the silver, the jewels, the mineral resources, the houses, the land, the livestock, the fields, the commodities, etc.

Wear your *wealth garment* with a sense of pride, because your heavenly Father gave it to you. Testify of His goodness and His blessings with absolutely no remorse and no sorrow.

This *Declaration Journey* story shows us how we have to battle to fight against the voices of others and change our thinking about what wealth will bring to us and upon us. God's blessings cannot be diluted from their greatness. Sorrow attempts to weaken the blessings of God, but we are overcomers and will not allow sorrow to be added or tacked on to our blessings.

Decree that you walk in joy concerning the blessings of The Lord. Decree that sorrow is an enemy, and it is cursed at the root. Declare you will no longer listen to voices of sorrow, but only the voice of Truth. Declare the joy in riches and wealth will flood your soul. Declare peace will rest upon your mind when it comes to the blessings of The Lord. Declare that no burden, no stress, and no misfortunes are tied to your money.

Declaration 9
Write your personal strategy to reject burdens attaching to your financial blessings.

DECLARATION 10

In Jesus name.

John 14:13-14
And whatever you ask in My name, that I will do, that the Father may be glorified in the Son. If you ask anything in My name, I will do it.

Where is the power of the name of Jesus in your heart? Have you embraced the real power of His name?

There is no other name under heaven given among men by which we must be saved (Acts 4:12); even the demons are subject to us at the name of Jesus (Luke 10:17); everyone who calls on the name of Jesus will be saved (Romans 10:13); in the name of Jesus Christ of Nazareth, rise up and walk (Acts 3:6); if you

123

ask anything in my name, I will do it (John 14:14; 16:26); in my name they will cast out demons; they will speak in new tongues (Mark 16:17); go therefore and make disciples of all nations, baptizing them in the name of the Father, of the Son and of the Holy Spirit (Matthew 28:19). These are just a few clips from scriptures to share the power of the name of Jesus. Asking what we are declaring in the name of Jesus is an instruction with promise. This power is not ours by accident, it is by divine planning. God has made Jesus the gateway to our provision through salvation. Without the work of Jesus Christ, we have no access to the fullness of what we are sharing in this book. So, to receive the

124

complete work, we must accept God's gift and blessing of Jesus Christ as Savior and Lord. This is the ultimate giving package. God gave so the world could receive and flourish through His seed He planted in the earth (John 3:16).

Holy Spirit is the teacher and revealer of truth. The truth is...wealth belongs to the children of God, and the children of God should reign with God's Word, Wisdom, and Wealth.

Declaration 10 Journey
Calling on the Name of Jesus (both authors)

Even though this is the last declaration, it is the
entry point to all of the declarations. Without
access to God and the resources of Heaven, we
would not have access to command our money
with divine authority. Salvation is calling on
the name of Jesus and a set up for eternal
success. We have both cried out to Jesus on
numerous *(continuous)* occasions. If you call
on Jesus, He promises to answer.

This declaration is to strengthen the validity
and the power of the name of Jesus in our
lives. So, with this declaration, we share
salvation. If you have not yet received Jesus as

Lord and Savior, we want you to do it NOW. Just repeat the words in the *Prayer of Access* with sincerity.

We are a people who belong to God, and He has made many great provisions for us. Let's begin to receive every provision and fully walk in the divine calling and purpose of The Lord.

Prayer of Access (Salvation)

Lord Jesus, I am a sinner and I repent of my sins. I make You the Lord of my life and I surrender my mind, heart, and soul to You. Teach me Your ways, lead me, and I will follow. Plant me in Your Word and govern my life.

I confess with my mouth and believe in my heart that You are the Son of God sent to save the world, that You died for my sins, and God raised You from the dead. I will work in Your vineyard until You return. Help me to walk in the fullness of Your promises and plan.

I thank You for keeping me on Your mind and that my name is written in the Lamb's book of Life. In YOUR (Jesus) name, Amen.

This *Declaration Journey* is all about access and how God has strategically placed it all in front of us through Jesus Christ. The fullness of *Commanding Your Money* lies in the pillar of salvation.

In the power of the name of Jesus, we receive boldness and confidence in the Word. In the power of the name of Jesus, we can reach beyond our borders into that which is borderless to God. The name of Jesus makes signs, wonders, and miracles available. The name of Jesus takes the limitations off of our natural mindset.

The price has been paid for our access. Do not let the price paid for treasured benefits be lost to you and your generations. Step over into the wealthy place and know you only got there because of the grace of God. Declare you are *wealth* and you cannot be separated from yourself.

Declaration 10
Write your personal strategy to reflect on the power of Jesus' name.

GETTING IN THE FLOW
Psalm 37:19

Understanding the streams of economic success has been underutilized and minimized by Believers. While the world has capitalized on the greater, we have sat back, for the most part, and become spectators. It's time to get in the game and produce for the sake of the Kingdom. Financial wealth is a neutralizer and a stabilizer for expansion, protection, and vision. Having money is NOT a sin! Let's repeat it together...Having money is NOT a sin. It is, however, one's pitfall to want money only for one's own pleasure and benefit. The love of money leads to one's demise. So, the correct understanding is that the 'love' of money IS the root of evil but having money as a tool to get you to God's destination is NOT.

Our mindset of money makes the difference. Let's examine how getting in the right streams can help us produce and sustain money flows. God's plan is to show us access, handling, and retention of money.

We are sharing seven (7) characteristics to successful streams. Think about your mindset for each stream characteristic. What can you implement, change, and strategize to flow in the right streams.

STREAM CHARACTERISTIC 1

The right stream can save you from starvation.

1 Kings 17:1-5
[Elijah drinks from the brook and is fed by ravens.]

In the middle of disaster and calamity, our streams will not run dry. If you are not in the right stream, you will not be able to partake in God's life-giving property. If you are not positioned in the right place, the same water that will give you life can be the same water that can take away your life. The same water that can heal you can be the same water that can kill you. Especially if you go into deep waters, and you don't know how to maneuver in the water God has sent you to.

Our success in life and our ability to strive in life is reliant on us being connected and positioned to the right supernatural stream.

God will give us direction to find the stream that will sustain us even in a drought. In the midst of your dry place or transition, when you're trying to figure out where to land, we can plainly ask God to show us our stream. We need a revelation of where our streams are. It's not about God showing us the money, but it's about God showing us our streams that will never run dry. When He shows it to us, we have to have the sense to declare, *'our streams will never run dry.'* We have to be in the right stream to produce. We cannot produce if we are not in the right good land and fertile ground.

We can go a long time without food, but we need water to survive. We can't just say God show me my stream, but we have to say God show me my stream that will save me. Show me a stream that will give me life and sustain me.

STREAM CHARACTERISTIC 2

The right stream will create multiple streams.

Genesis 2:10
[A river went out of Eden to water the garden; and parted and became four.]

When we are positioned at the right stream, we will begin to see new streams and more streams. The streams in Eden did not run dry, because they went to four different places.

We have to believe if we are positioned by the right stream, it will create more streams for us. We can't believe it if we don't see it. So, we have to pay attention to those who are multiplying. If we get caught up in a stream and there's a bunch of people and there is only one stream for all of us, sooner or later that stream is going to run dry. But we have to declare our streams shall not run dry.

STREAM CHARACTERISTIC 3

The right stream will produce the right fruit.

Matthew 7:17-20
[They will know you by the fruit you bear.]

You can tell when there is not a right stream or fertile land, because fruit won't grow. When people have asked us who should be their mentor, we say become a fruit inspector to see what kind of fruit they are producing. If we are by the right stream, we can't help but produce the right fruit.

Perverted streams produce perverted fruit. This is why we have to know those with whom we labor with, and know if they are connected to the right stream. The right stream will produce the right fruit, and the right fruit will produce after its own kind. The right fruit can do what cannot be done by compromised fruit. Find others who are producing the right fruit. Ask God to show you someone who knows how to produce and multiply in dry places, in troubled times, under pressure; because they will easily be able to produce in good times.

STREAM CHARACTERISTIC 4

The right stream will lead to new streams.

John 4:1-10
[The well of Jacob, led the Samaritan woman to a much deeper well.]

When you follow the path of the right stream, it will lead you to the path of a new stream. When it leads you to a new stream, we can declare, *'our streams will never run dry.'* When we are closely connected to the right stream, it produces a new stream when we least expect it. When we are connected to the right stream, multiplication is our portion. When we are connected to the right stream, the right fruit is our portion and inside the right fruit is the right seed. The right seed in the fruit will produce another stream. This is why we have to examine the kind of people around us and know what kind of fruit they are producing. If the fruit is authentic, we can plant the seed to produce. If the fruit is contaminated, the seed can die before anyone touches it. We also have to ask the question of ourselves, what type of fruit are we producing? If we produce the right fruit, we can take our own seed and plant it, and it will germinate and grow into a new stream.

STREAM CHARACTERISTIC 5

The right stream will lead to the right supplier.

1 Kings 17:1-5
[Elijah's drought led him to a place of provision.]

Listening to God will direct us to the right stream, and at the right stream we will receive the right suppliers. Sometimes we may be connected with those we would not normally associate with to get to a new and right stream. We can be positioned to leverage our loss with unusual association to get in the flow of a stream. Don't get caught up with who the supplier is, but focus on what God is doing for

144

us. With the right supplier, we don't have to work as hard to receive the blessing.

The raven is considered a nasty bird, but it was the supplier of Elijah's food in the time of need. God will use what and who He needs to use to get what needs to be done. If Elijah had gotten caught up in the raven being a nasty bird and refused the bread he was bringing, he could have starved to death. For a season and a reason, God may send us into a place to receive what we need from the world and even from the wicked. If that be the case, we maintain the character of a Believer to bear witness to God's glory and use the opportunity to plant seeds to harvest souls.

STREAM CHARACTERISTIC 6

When one stream dries up, there is always another one.

1 Kings 17:7-14
[When it's dry, it's dry...move on to the next stream.]

God always has another one waiting for us. If a stream ends, don't panic, we can ask God to help us discover another one. There is always a stream we forgot about, or we have never noticed. God is able to call life to come forth concerning our streams. He is able to do exceedingly, abundantly above all we can ask, think or imagine according to the power that works on the inside of us. The same way He allowed the stream to dry up is the same way

He will position you to a new stream. When one dries up, we can say, *'there has got to be another one.'*

STREAM CHARACTERISTIC 7

The right wind will release the right water stream.

Ecclesiastes 4:9-12
[Working together.]

Sometimes we never know how heavy the flow can be until the right wind comes. We don't understand how hard the rain is falling until all of a sudden the wind comes. Make sure you are positioned in a place when the winds come to receive what they bring as the right stream to be released in your life supernaturally. Some people get caught up in a dry place and are afraid to shift or move even if it's not producing. The right wind will release the right water over our lives. We are walking in

148

increase and at a higher level, because we are moving with the winds of change in the right stream.

Pay attention to what's going on around you; where to invest; what to do next; have a vision and look at the vision of others (we all flow together). Collaboration during the winds of change will give us the opportunity to rise together. We can connect with the right people and flow in streams together to gain greater strength.

THE WORD AND MONEY

The following scriptures taken from the Holy Bible (NKJV) connect us to biblical principles of money. We have given the book with the verse(s) and a summary thought for some and the actual scriptures for others.

We recommend you look up each scripture for yourself to reflect on each one for reading and meditation. As we mentioned before, there are many money scriptures. Be encouraged to seek the scriptures to find more. It is worth the time to study the Word and put these scriptures in your heart. It will create a well you will be able to draw from when needed. Once it is planted in your memory bank of the mind and heart, you give it the right to be brought back to your remembrance.

MONEY WEALTH SCRIPTURES

Honor God by learning what He says about money, riches, and wealth.

Deuteronomy 8:18
And you shall remember the Lord your God, for it is He who gives you power to get wealth, that He may establish His covenant which He swore to your fathers, as it is this day.

1 Chronicles 29:14
But who am I, and who are my people, That we should be able to offer so willingly as this? For all things come from You, And Your own we have given You.

Proverbs 18:16
A man's gift makes room for him, And brings him before great men.

Proverbs 11:25
A generous soul will be made rich, And he who waters will also be watered himself.

2 Corinthians 8:12
For if there is first a willing mind, it is accepted according to what one has, and not according to what he does not have.

Luke 6:38
Give and it will be given to you; good measure, pressed down, shaken together, and running over will be put into your bosom. For with the same measure that you use, it will be measured back to you.

Proverbs 3:9
Honor the Lord with your possessions, and with the firstfruits of all your increase.

2 Corinthians 9:10
Now may He who supplies seed to the sower, and bread for food, supply and multiply the seed you have sown and increase the fruits of your righteousness,

2 Corinthians 9:8
And God is able to make all grace abound toward you, that you, always having all sufficiency in all things, may have an abundance for every good work.

Proverbs 3:27
Do not withhold good from those to whom it is due, When it is the power of your hand to do so.

Malachi 3:10
Bring all the tithes into the storehouse, That there may be food in My house, And try Me now in this," Says the Lord of hosts, "If I will not open for you the windows of heaven And pour out for you such blessing That there will not be room enough to receive it.

Luke 6:30
Give to everyone who asks of you. And from him who takes away your goods do not ask them back.

Psalm 37:4
Delight yourself also in the Lord, And He shall give you the desires of your heart.

Proverbs 21:26
He covets greedily all day long, But the righteous gives and does not spare.

Matthew 6:2
Therefore, when you do a charitable deed, do not sound a trumpet before you as the hypocrites do in the synagogues and in the streets, that they may have glory from men. Assuredly, I say to you, they have their reward.

Matthew 19:21
Jesus said to him, "If you want to be perfect, go, sell what you have and give to the poor, and you will have treasure in heaven; and come, follow Me."

1 Corinthians 13:3
And though I bestow all my goods to feed the poor, and though I give my body to be burned, but have not love, it profits me nothing.

Psalm 37:21
The wicked borrows and does not repay, But the righteous shows mercy and gives.

Matthew 10:8
Heal the sick, cleanse the lepers, raise the dead, cast out demons. Freely you have received, freely give.

Proverbs 31:9
Open your mouth, judge righteously, And plead the cause of the poor and needy.

Matthew 6:3-4
But when you do a charitable deed, do not let your left hand know what your right hand is doing, that your charitable deed may be in secret; and your Father who sees in secret will Himself reward you openly.

Proverb 13:22
A good man leaves an inheritance to his children's children, But the wealth of the sinner is stored up for the righteous.

Matthew 6:24
No one can serve two masters; for either he will hate the one and love the other, or else he will be loyal to the one and despise the other. You cannot serve God and mammon.

Luke 16:11
Therefore if you have not been faithful in the unrighteous mammon, who will commit to your trust the true riches?

MONEY CONCEPT SCRIPTURES

If we are unfaithful with handling our money, it will affect our relationship with God.

Psalm 24:1
[God owns everything.]

Matthew 4:4
[Man should live by the Word of God.]

2 Timothy 3:16-17
[All scripture is given by God.]

Deuteronomy 8:18
[God gives power to get wealth.]

Proverbs 3:7:10
[Honor the Lord with what is given to you, and you will have more than enough.]

Luke 6:38
[Give a little and receive a little.]

Malachi 3:8-10
[Will you attempt to rob God?]

Matthew 25
[Steward...to manage over the property of others, you must be able to manage your own.]

Proverb 13:18, 22
[Will we listen and follow instructions from God concerning our finances?]

Romans 10:9
[Salvation and acceptance of Jesus' teachings gives us access to financial wisdom.]

Matthew 6:24
[Will we serve God with money we possess, or will we serve only ourselves with money we possess?]

Luke 16:11
[Can you be trusted with true wealth?]

Isaiah 55:8-9
[Learn God's ways of handling money; they are different from our ways of handling money.]

1 Chronicles 29:11-12
[Reflect on God's ownership; give God the credit for what He has done.]

Deuteronomy 10:14
[God owns everything, and He gives those He loves access to use it.]

1 Corinthians 10:26
[Gain, all things belong to God.]

Leviticus 25:23
[We occupy what God owns.]

Psalm 50:10-12
[Every living thing and resource belongs to God.]

Haggai 2:8
[Every precious metal and jewel belong to God.]

MONEY REFLECTION SCRIPTURES

NO LACK
Psalm 34:9-10; Matthew 6:31-33; Philippians 4:19
God has promised to provide for us and take care of our needs if we seek Him first.

GOOD STEWARD
1 Corinthians 4:2; Luke 16:1-2; Luke 16:10
God rewards a good steward.

DEBT
Proverbs 22:7; Deuteronomy 15:4-6; Deuteronomy 28:1-2, 12; Deuteronomy 18:15, 43-45; Romans 13:8; 1 Corinthians 7:23; Psalm 37:21; Proverbs 3:27-28
Debt can be considered a curse when it makes you a slave to systems and men. If you have debt, take care of it because if you don't, it can ruin your reputation and your living.

SEEK COUNSEL BEFORE YOU ACT
2King 4:1-7; Proverbs 22:26-27; Proverbs 17:18; Proverbs 6:1-5; Proverbs 12:15; Proverbs 13:10; Proverbs 15:22; Psalm 16:7; Psalm 32:8; Psalm 106:13-15
Undesirable things can happen when we don't seek the counsel of God and those He appoints as true ambassadors.

UNSHAKEABLE INTEGRITY
Leviticus 19:11; Leviticus 19:11-13; Deuteronomy 25:13-16; Ephesians 4:25; 1 Peter 1:15-16; Proverbs 28:16; Proverbs 12:22; Proverbs 20:7; Isaiah 33:15-16; Proverbs 3:32; Proverbs 13:11; Proverbs 21:6; Exodus 22:1-4; Numbers 5:5-8; Luke 19:8; Exodus 23:8 Proverbs 15:27; Proverbs 29:4
Integrity offers speed in negotiations and deals.

GIVE GENEROUSLY
Luke 12:34; Acts 20:35; Matthew 23:23; 1 Corinthians 13:3; 2 Corinthians 9:7; Acts 20:35; Proverbs 11:24-25; Matthew 6:20; Malachi 3:8-10; 2 Corinthians 8:1-5; Numbers 18:8-10; 24; Galatians 6:6; 1 Timothy 5:17-18; Isaiah 58:6-11; Ezekiel 16:49; Matthew 25:35-45; Galatians 2:9-10; Colossians 3:23-24
Imitate God in being a generous giver.

WORK HARD
Genesis 2:15; Genesis 3:17-19; Exodus 20:9; 2 Thessalonians 3:10-12; Genesis 39:2-5; Exodus 35:30-35; Exodus 36:1-2; Psalm 75:6-7; Ephesians 6:5-9; Colossians 3:22-25; 1 Peter 2:18; Proverbs 18:9; 2 Thessalonians 3:7-9; Exodus 34:21; Proverbs 31:10-28; Titus 2:4-5
Working hard and being honest bring good character.

PLANS TO PROSPER

Proverbs 21:5; Genesis 41:34-36; Proverbs 21:20; Luke 12:16-21, 34; 1 Timothy 5:8; 1 Timothy 6:9-10; Proverbs 24:27; Proverbs 27:23-24; Ecclesiastes 3:1; Genesis 24:35-36; Proverbs 13:22; 2 Corinthians 12:14; Proverbs 20:21; Galatians 4:1-2; Proverbs 28:20-22; Philippians 4:11-13; Deuteronomy 30:15-16; Joshua 1:8

God has a plan to prosper whatever you put your hands to. What are your hands working on?

CONTENTMENT AND FAITH

Hebrews 11:36-40; Job 1:8-21; Genesis 37:23-28; 39:7-20; 1 Timothy 6:6-8; 2 Corinthians 11:23-27; Psalm 73:1-20; Philippians 4:11-13; Job 36:11

Be content while having faith for greater.

COMMUNITY MONEY
Matthew 5:25-26; Romans 13:1-7; James 2:1-9; Romans 12:16; Philippians 2:3; Acts 4:32-37; 1 Thessalonians 4:11-12; Deuteronomy 6:6-7; Proverbs 22:6; Ephesians 6:4
Our wealth is not just for us.

ETERNAL MONEY CONCEPTS
Mark 8:36; Psalm 39:4-6; Psalm 103:13-16; Psalm 90:10-12; 1 Chronicles 29:15; Philippians 3:20; 1 Peter 2:11; 2 Peter 3:10-13; Ecclesiastes 12:13-14; 2 Corinthians 5:9-10; 1 Corinthians 3:11-15; 2 Corinthians 4:18
Build your hopes and foundation on eternal things. Make your 'money mark' in God's Kingdom.

MONEY NUGGETS

Learn what God says about money. It will give you an eternal and Kingdom perspective.

Create a Godly attitude about money. It will keep you safe and protected from the love of a thing that can't love you back.

Give all your money direction, so satanic worms won't eat it up.

God understands the efforts of money. When we understand God's principle and purpose of money, we will use money with a different heart and mindset.

God created the idea of wealth, because He created what generates wealth.

Everything that belongs to God is valuable, therefore we must put value on it.

It doesn't matter how much money you start with, you can have a successful financial future if you have a healthy biblically-based money mindset.

There is no such thing as spare change, because all my money has an assignment.

If you don't decide where your money will go, it will go where others want it to go.

Don't waste your money on things that do not bring value to your money mindset.

Put yourself in the learning wealth academy you create. Take every opportunity to get the 412 (that's a step higher than the 411) on money matters. When something is important to you, you will make and take the time to devote the necessary attention to nurture it.

The money/wealth gain is not just for your benefit, but it's to put you in the posture to function and operate in God's economy. *Having* houses, land deals, contracts, businesses puts the Believer in a position to represent godly wealth practices.

Attract money opportunities by leveraging multiple streams of income. One door will open a door to another door.

Learn money terminology, methodology, and psychology. In all your getting, get understanding about what you want to be successful in.

Confess that you are *wealth,* and you cannot be separated from yourself.

When you demand more of yourself, you will see more success.

Act like you have what you want before you get it.

Be a practitioner of wisdom so you can produce wealth.

Let your giving be a reflection of your harvest.

Let your motives for money be the reason to increase your wealth.

Think giving...Where can I sow to make a Kingdom difference?

5 MONEY POSITION PRAYERS

Prayer for Faith and Wealth

Dear God, we thank You for increasing the faith and the wealth of Your people. God, we thank You that their faith is increased at a level that will cause wealth to be their portion. So even now, God, we bind up anything that will come directly to hinder their faith and hinder their wealth; anything that would cause them to think that You're not able to create wealth in them. God we come against the spirit of doubt and everything that would try to cancel faith out. God, I prophesy that their faith is increased on this day. I prophesy that even as they have faith the size of a mustard seed, they can say to the mountain of doubt, 'be thou removed.' I thank You, God, that even as they move forward in this new season of their life, that their faith will be increased and their wealth will be increased like never before. God, I thank You that those who look at them will be able to see the transformation. And, God, I thank You there will be obvious transformations over them as they move into this new dispensation in time. So, God, we thank You for an increase in faith and wealth. In Jesus name, Amen

Prayer for a Wealth Mindset

Father, We thank You for this time of commanding money. You are changing our mindsets about wealth. We are evolving in our thinking, and Your voice is the louder voice in our heads. We thank You that we have a mindset of believing what is Truth. We thank You that we have the mind of Christ. We are wrapped in a spirit of wealth and so are our minds.

We come against all negativity that has been placed in us, and we uproot it so that it is no more. We thank You for the power of the mind. We thank You for giving us the ability to choose and make decisions. We ask that our decisions are in divine alignment with Your mind and Your heart. We thank You that our mindsets regarding our wealth are mindsets You have established and nothing can interfere or take it from us. Our minds are made up and we stand firmly on Your Word and what You say about our wealth. In Jesus name, Amen.

Prayer for Ability to Create Wealth

God, Your Word tells us You have given us the power to create wealth. So, we stand on your power today. And we declare and decree that your people shall be able to move forth with the spirit of creativity that leads to wealth. We thank You, God, that their minds are expanded to the level that it needs to be so that they can believe indeed there is creative power on the inside of them for wealth. And, so God we thank You now for creativity, ingenuity, and we thank You, God, for causing wealth to be their position. God we thank you for new businesses, we thank you for new ideas, and new streams coming forth that will lead to wealth. And, God we plead the blood of Jesus

174

over them and declare and decree, no weapon formed against their wealth shall be able to prosper. Every word and tongue that rises up against their wealth they shall be able to condemn. God, we come in agreement with their creativity, we prophesy creativity upon them, the spirit of creativity that rests in You; God we also ask that it rests in each and every one of them. In Jesus name, Amen.

Prayer for Generational Wealth and Wisdom

Father, In the name of Jesus, we decree and declare we are indeed the seed of Abraham, and his seed is blessed in such a measure that it would be a blessing to the nations. On this day, we are blessed to be a blessing to the nations. We pray that the anointing falls upon us so our eyes will be opened to see who we are and whose we are. We are joint heirs of Jesus Christ and partakers of the Abrahamic covenant. The covenant that breaks the curse of poverty and the covenant that makes us the lender and not the borrower. Let us receive this anointing, let us receive this inheritance, that birthright of all those who believe. Let all our generations flow in wealth and have the wisdom to manage it. We speak Your wisdom over our lives and over our future generations. In Jesus name, Amen.

Prayer Commands for Businesses

Dear God, I command my business to line up to produce wealth.

I command every aspect of my business to line up with the word of God.

I command contracts and relationships to bring abundance.

I command my movement in the marketplace to create divine portals that cause supernatural rivers of wealth to flow in my business and in my career.

I thank You, God, for expanding my mindset regarding my business and my career; and as I move forward, thank You God for showing me how to command my money in every aspect of my life.

As I command my money I thank You for the power to get wealth.
In Jesus name, Amen

REFLECTIONS

As you reflect on what God says about your money in the scriptures, the declarations, the streams, the prayers, etc., you will develop a stronger confidence in God and the operation of your faith when it comes to money. You will begin to *think about what you're thinking about.*

Whatever you have and wherever you are right now, stop and bless it. What you have to offer, bless it, and pray over it. Offer it to God and ask Him to multiply and increase it. You cannot accomplish what we are challenging you to do and become without living under God's principles, walking with Jesus Christ, and receiving wisdom and revelation from Holy Spirit.

Creating a true lifestyle of *Commanding Your Money* will also breed a lifestyle of right thinking. As we declare and decree over our money out of our mouths, our thinking will become a force in the Kingdom that we will not only be able to *speak a thing*, but we will be able to *think a thing* and it will manifest.

We strongly encourage you to take what we are sharing in this book seriously and become a practitioner of what is being preached. Remember, this is about *sowing first*. Have a heart to give abundantly for the purpose of God, and seed will be given for the purpose of sowing (2 Corinthians 9:10). In this same fashion, people will give to you the commodities of time, talent, and treasure.

Let your mindset be a student of the spirit of exposure and the spirit of abundance. Remember, we are not servants of money, but money serves us. Develop a lifestyle and habit of *Commanding Your Money*.

ABOUT THE AUTHORS

Above all other things, we are women of faith. We both have extensive backgrounds in ministry and honor God in our personal living and businesses. We are accomplished ministers of the Gospel of Jesus Christ, authors, speakers, and trainers.

This book is one of many books we have written designed to help the Body of Christ understand, put into practice, and walk in the fullness of God's Word not only concerning money, but calling, anointing, living, and the blessings of the Lord.

We are not professional financial advisors, but we are stewards who operate in the promises of God concerning money.

We are encouragers and seek to empower God's people to know God's Word works in their lives. If we live under the obedience of God as His people, He promises we will flourish even in the wilderness.

DWANN HOLMES is former broadcast journalist, and is known as a Media Mentor to many. She is an award-winning journalist, Emmy-nominated producer, inspirational speaker, crisis solutionist, and marketing executive called to leverage leaders into new levels of Kingdom Manifestation. She has combined her 20+ year media background with ministerial insight to show God's 5-fold ministry leaders and pastors how to easily evangelize on and offline.

As Founder of the Global Institute of Church and Marketplace Prophets (GICMP), Dwann is a prophetic authority to the nations called to set order and build systems of accountability for God's Kingdom mouthpieces across the world. Dwann is also the Founder and Lead Pastor of Global Prophetic Life Training & Worship Embassy.

In April 2001 Ebony Magazine named her 1 of 30 future leaders of America aged 30 and under.

Whether in the pulpit or auditorium, Dwann walks in miracles, signs, and wonders bringing healing, hope, and prophetic revelation to all, particularly those called to marketplace ministry and prophetics.

ROSEMARY WINBUSH is a minister, author, speaker, consultant, blogger/producer, and mentor focusing on women, children, and families. She is gifted in helping others reach their maximum divine potential through the Word of God, self-evaluation, developing directional tracks, and producing results that yield success. Rosemary has worked with children and families for more than 30 years. She has over 30 years of ministry leadership and 19 years of ministerial staffing experience.

She has authored spiritually based help books, and marriage tools, and produced inspirational healing and affirmation albums. Rosemary has leveraged her expertise to assist families develop better home environments to promote family maturity, spiritual growth, and healthy living.

Rosemary is the founding host of the *BEST Me* project for students and *The7Movement* bible study project for women. She is a recipient of the R. David and I. Lorraine Thomas Child Advocate of the Year award.

Rosemary is a trainer and coach to ministry and business leadership teams. She has presented at conferences, private business groups, workshops, and preached at worship services.

PASTOR
Rosemary Winbush
Kairos International
Minister, Speaker, Author, and Trainer,
Success Coach and Life Builder for
Children's Ministry Leader's and Workers,
Families, Church Leaders, People
Essentials to START, BUILD, REFRESH
CHILDREN'S MINISTRY
Baby Dedication
Bible Snapshot
Journey Through the Word
Essentials to
Start Build and Refresh
Children's Ministry
Baby Dedication:
It's Not About the Baby
Bible SnapShot:
Journey Through the Word
LIVE
AFFIRMATIONS
Available at
amazon
Live Healing
for Children
Affirmations
www.rosemarywinbush.com

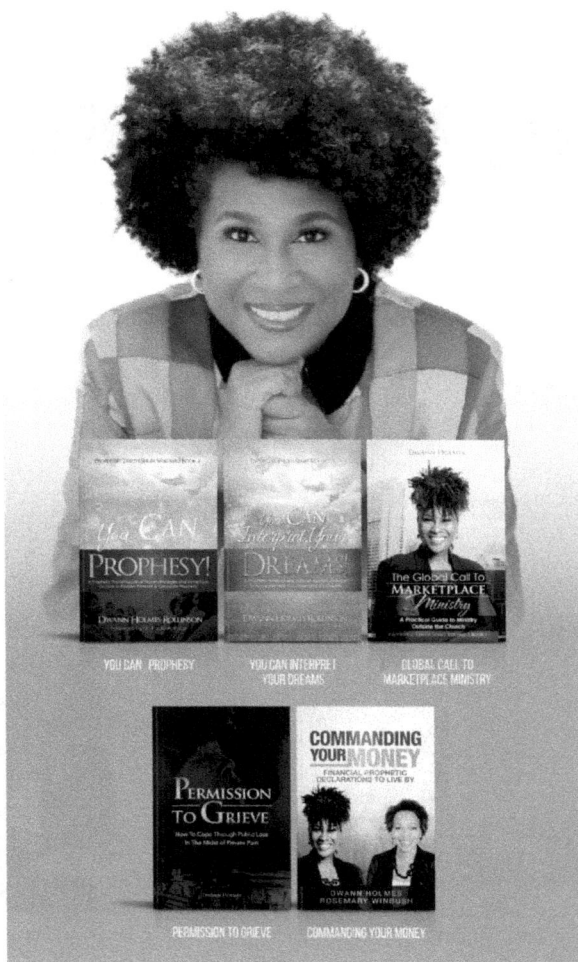

YOU CAN PROPHESY

YOU CAN INTERPRET YOUR DREAMS

GLOBAL CALL TO MARKETPLACE MINISTRY

PERMISSION TO GRIEVE

COMMANDING YOUR MONEY

The Global Call To
MARKETPLACE
Ministry
GICMP
PROPHETS
Join me on clubhouse in my
MASTER
MARKETPLACE
Ministry
CLUB